THE ICE LIZARD

PREVIOUS BOOKS (1969–79) PUBLISHED UNDER THE NAME
JUDITH JOHNSON SHERWIN:

Uranium Poems (Yale University Press, 1969)
(Yale Series of Younger Poets Prize)

The Life of Riot: short stories (Atheneum, 1970)

Impossible Buildings: poems (Doubleday, 1972)

The Waste Trilogy: poems (Countryman Press)
The Town Scold (1977)
Transparencies (1978)
Dead's Good Company (1979)

How the Dead Count: poems (Norton, 1978)

NON-FICTION:

Literary Agents: a complete guide (Poets & Writers, 1978)

AUDIO-BOOK:

The Town Scold (Watershed Tapes, 1977)

FORTHCOMING:

Hungry for Light: The Journal of Ethel Schwabacher
ed. Judith E. Johnson and Brenda S. Webster
(Indiana University Press, 1993)

for Renata
in the empty end
pretty of sisterhood
Judy

THE ICE LIZARD

POEMS 1977–88

by

Judith Emlyn Johnson

The Sheep Meadow Press
Riverdale-on-Hudson, New York

I am grateful to the National Endowment for the Arts for a fellowship, and to the State University of New York at Albany for a grant of released time, which made it possible to complete this book.

I am also grateful to the many friends and family members who have, over the years, suggested revisions for some of the poems in this book: Carolyn Kizer, Jean Anaporte, Marilyn Hacker, Edgar and Eleanor Johnson, Miranda, Alison, and Galen Sherwin, and my editor, Stanley Moss.

All inquiries and permission requests should be addressed to: The Sheep Meadow Press, P. O. Box 1345, Riverdale-on-Hudson, New York 10471.

Distributed by Independent Literary Publishers Association
        P. O. Box 816
        Oak Park, IL 60603

Typeset in Mergenthaler Bembo by Keystrokes, Lenox, Massachusetts Printed by Princeton University Press on acid-free paper. It meets the guidelines for permanence and durability of the Committee on Production Guidelines for Book Longevity of the Council on Library Resources.

Library of Congress Cataloging-in-Publication Data

Johnson, Judith Emlyn.
    The ice lizard : poems 1977–88 / by Judith Emlyn Johnson.
      p.   cm.
    ISBN 1-878818-17-1 (acid-free) : $12.95
    I. Title.
PS3560.037953I28   1992
811'.54—dc20   92-17133
                                             CIP

to my mother and father
Eleanor and Edgar Johnson
this book is lovingly dedicated
for your love that wrote me

TABLE OF CONTENTS

PART ONE: WAKING

PART TWO: GRAND MAJESTIC STOMP

PART THREE: THE VIGIL

PART FOUR: WHAT THE RAIN TAKES

ACKNOWLEDGMENTS

I am grateful to the editors of the following periodicals and anthologies, who accepted for publication, sometimes in different forms and under different titles, the following poems:

The America-Italy Conference Book: "Perspectives" (published in Italy)
Asphodel: "Fable of the Date Trees"
The Bloomsday Anthology: "The Immortality of the Hotrod," "The Normal"
Caprice: "Snorkle," "Report on the Experiment 'Romulus 9' "
Chelsea: "Wuzzit" (with performance score), "Surrounded by Jerks," "In Jane's Red Room"
Confrontation: "Before Notre Dame: What the Rain Takes," "Before Notre Dame: In Leaping Green"
Frontiers: "The Ice Lizard" (the four poems, separate in this collection, appeared together as one four part poem)
The Glens Falls Review: "Beachcombing"
Groundswell: "Eastern Amusements," "Things of the House," "The Party After Antony," "Snow on a Moonless Night,"[1] "Before Notre Dame: Whatever I've Taken"
Letters Home: "Canticle of the Foreign Wars"
The Literary Review: "A Slow Measure"
The Little Magazine: "Some Far Place"
Milkweed Chronicle: "Marchers of Ragnarok: Bifrost," "Poem of Negative Density" (under the title "Words Like Balloons, Words Like Smoke, Words Like Seeds")
Ms.: "The End of Love"
The New York Times Op-Ed Page: "Foreign Exchange Blues"
The New Yorker: "Ballade of the Grindstones"[2]
North Country Anthology: "Calling It Right," "Taking Stock"

[1]reprinted in *Gates to the City,* ed. Jeanne Finley, et al.
[2]reprinted in *Strong Measures,* ed. Philip Dacey and David Jauss

Oovrah: "Perspectives" (first American publication), "Jérôme Bosch, in Gent, Contemplates New York Street Life"
The Partisan Review: "Body Politic"
A Shout in the Street: "A Grief Beyond Remedy"
The Southwest Review: "Steenweg"
Struga Poetry Festival Publication: "Whoopee"
The Virginia Quarterly Review: "Before the Recovery"
WomanPoet-the East: "Miranda's Birthspell"

Poetry: "Marchers of Ragnarok: The Spoilers and the Spoils"[3]
("Marchers of Ragnarok: The Spoilers and the Spoils" first appeared in *Poetry*. Copyright 1978 by The Modern Poetry Association. Reprinted by permission of the editor of *Poetry*)

[3]reprinted in *Strong Measures*

PART ONE: WAKING

"I dreamed I circled Manhattan in my Maidenform™ bra"

WAKING THE ICE LIZARD

for Jean Easton Anaporte

Well past the midpoint of my life, not in a dark
wood, but in my own house, eyes closed, i went downstairs
to the sub-basement / where i thought i remembered
a stonewalled root cellar. There, in the deadening calm
that comes of making no waves, i felt shiver, deep
      in the mist, embedded
in the uneven stones i touched at the back wall,
      in a coil, big as a room,
      older than Lascaux,
         something,
           she,
              the Ice Lizard
whom i had so long forgotten
and had come there to wake.
The air held
      a limestone   sweat   smell.

Her coiled, knotted backbone beaded
under the etched scales. Above the bony knots, folded
from browbone to tailspines, flat against her scales,
rested her knife-edged backridges. Her green, thick
      ridged   tail   stretched   miles
into the ice age under us, grew into that rock.
As she opened one yellow eye and saw me, her backplates sprang
                         up like sails.
      Both eyes open now
      she uncoiled her arched
           swan
             proud
               maned
                 sweeping

racehorse neck. Her nostrils
flared   smoked
with primeval cold.

Do you need me? she croaked, stretching her claws,
kneading the stone flags.

                    Yes, ice lady, i answered. *I came here*
to wake you. Lead me down your dark.

                    Then she uncoiled
her thick neck, swung her head back down over
my eyes. *Open,* she hissed. Her cold tongue
flicked my forehead, my cheeks.
I've been waiting for you, she said.

MOON AS MILLSTONE

Mother mother sleep tonight
don't count how many days are left

last night your moon milled the shadows under these trees
which were hungry and ate them.
my three girls watched the night dream
i've forgotten anything i knew about survival

earth / moon
don't   look   down
tell me it won't happen.
The sun won't lean over to spoon white
beaten
clouds
into your mouth
my three children will live forever.
They won't burn in this ash air
till their eyes boil and the clean white
moon sockets cry them down,
gully out their cheeks
with their lost years

it won't happen
we won't live to count the wounds of this quiet
earth   /   moon
who tenderly mills the shadows under the trees
and makes of them grain
and makes of them grain

JÉRÔME BOSCH, IN GENT, CONTEMPLATES NEW YORK STREET LIFE

1

COME back Jérôme Bosch they told me
from wherever it is you're at, but
i didn't pay no mind. First
because ain't no way back, next
because i don't know where *back*
or *you're at* is, last because
i ain't Jérôme Bosch.

2

Come back Jérôme Bosch they told me
first because we need
you to paint the scene real
bad here in the Apple, next
because *long time* sweet babe
no see those men with corkscrew eyes
open you up and then some, last
because for sure you ain't
him.

BEFORE THE RECOVERY

THIS room might have been an operating theater
before it became the field
where our hearts were raked over to find
why they died before we did. I could have told

the man in the white mask who stood just back of your ear
how much more to give in order to break
the rhythm of your farewell oration. You could have shown
my reading of the symptoms slipshod. How much did it take,

in the end, to put you out? Not much more than you felt
deaden the skin so the laser could cut in
and ease the one part of the brain we knew needed rest.
That white cauliflower of evil where speech had been

we severed. In the perfect solace we have made
we can ask the consulting pathologist whether the patient died
                                        for a song
he could not sing, whether the physician erred
in assessing both fault and fee. Before long

from the telephone booth whose lines are cut
i shall tell you what you think. Without a sound
to break your dumb certainty, you will tell me what
i think. We shall both be wrong.

In every court where the art of dead reckoning is known
the price we paid will be held fair.
Only when the skull, whose lid had been lifted with one edge of
                                        a knife, was shown
jiggling open to let the steam out, hissing, as it curled the hair

did i see how uncertain a gift it was to fix the cause.
How can i tell you what it was like,
that final and original departure of your voice
which once i loved?
                  The failure of love will make us die

as the mask filters this gas we call our air.
Can i say at the finish
i was there /
             when you were not there?

CALLING IT RIGHT

(for Joel Oppenheimer)

Out my window there's grass. The whole frame shakes
with subway trains. Sundays the children shout
the park up. I hear when the wood connects.
Though i have work to do, don't care for baseball,
don't mean to watch them hit and run, don't know
whose kids they are or whether they need watching,
my mind lets out an absent-minded whoop
when they do.
          Anything that can take off
and go like hell or land on base will need
a cheer to fix it steady. Too much can
fall short and does. The kids that i don't watch
whether they hit or miss may wind up hitting
or missing some time when i'll wish they hadn't.
Go down past those split benches some dark night,
the quick plock of feet will count how they run
and run when the whole park shouts out past counting
someone's kid just been hit.
          Tell me they'll strike
out or hit home whether i watch or not,
whether i do my work or not. Say others
will let them walk or call them safe. But still,
i can't get by so lightly. Something's out
there i should put my mind to if i knew
how i could call it right. For now, i'm not
all outside their game even though they're all in it,
nor are they any less out, being in
here and on base.
          Last night after the ninth,
the moon up, all kids home, their good time over,
i turned my light down and looked past the field

to where something came up the wall and sat.
Couldn't see what it was nor whether it
had scored, but only how it sat and sat
and looked past me while i looked out at it,
helpless to change its run of luck and yet
hoping next time i hit, it calls me right.

SPEAKERS

My mouth is opening again. Look, you can feel it stretch.
It utters a minnow. Whoops, it utters a whale.
It utters the mouth of a river, it utters a ketch
which it sends up the river, utters a fleet in full sail.
It spits out freight piled on the docksides. It chews out the night
closing in. It gapes, tells out streets, buses that cough,
that spurt through that throathole, that stutter to a stop at the light;
at the outer edge, utters the man with the knife, who chokes off
and spills out a life at the corner / his quicksilvered eyes,
the scales stuck tight over. It coins the new minted tails
of the minnows / coins, at the utterance, that fish which flies
from a bigger fish, crawls up the land, grabs a knife, prevails,
which covers the speaking earth from north to south
and prevails, which i didn't know i had in my mouth.

SNORKLE

1

Friends, it's like this: out of the bathtub
endlessly filling / i filled the tub last night
with green water, poured in
winesoap, diamonds, pinesap, pearls, oilslicks, teeth, what the
        hell, i just happened to have all those
        options lying around. So this
   chosen mix, in a glitter, came
        bubbling up from the neutral
   depths of the underground
        meltingpot. When i
poked in one conservative toe to test the neighborhood
        heat / silk
        streamers swirled all around. Then i plunged
             an investor, a real
             mogul,
        in, the whole foot—
something bit it off, whoops, i've been
had, something's scored off me, it's an
        alligator, a razorshell giant
            clam, a one hundred per cent white
        whale, the ravenous führer of all
        moray eels, it strikes, its head cresting the clean
        surface, the Blob, but with teeth, a city-size
            amoeba made
        of acids and wits.
          Great, jumping, greeneyed
toads, did I make that thing?

2
     No
way will you pin
that swamp thing on me / maybe the tub was mine (though
          you'd have to prove i held title to it) but the
         water sure wasn't, came right out of the faucet. Well, that
city water is hopping with junk / not my kind
             of bond or
responsibility / there's an aurora shimmying
       over the waterspout above the
       drain / there's
       steam weaving green ribbons up from this
       soup / the elements,
though i drew them into the tub, sure weren't my
mixture (which was bourbon and perrier).

3

       Let me tell you,
friends, there's something
waiting on the underside of the
bathwater / that turns things
mean. If i empty out
       this tub and draw another
       it's likely to send out lassoes, sar-
       gassoes, helixes
       doubled, redoubled into
       game / Some days there's just no safe
       place you can poke a toe
into. Make a move, buy into a good
district, and the wildlife bites back. I know some who have lost
       more than their shirts. The neighborhood is
       changing. What you put in
       you won't get back, unless you change
       your skin, and then you could find
       yourself growing in all that
slime and it growing in you, no purity left.

Yes, you could call that
mix a solution, but unless you're
into finalities, you're better unsolved. So tell the boys
from the great society: *scoobie-dee, scoobie-*
doo / i've been
had, but it ain't by
you, mister,   goo-
bye.

EASTERN AMUSEMENTS

Riverside, looking towards the Palisades

Sunset signed on the Palisades' dotted line
    where once roller coasters looped their signatures
                        round the sun
          i saw the bumper cars crash
thump when they struck memory.

Is the subway a god or a worm?
Is there a god in the worm or a worm in the god
that rattles me uptown to the end of the line?
Is there a river
        is there firm ground which is not the same ground
as the river?
        If i ride these rails
through this bedrocked Manhattan Schist[1]
                out of Manhattan Night
    and on into the greater night, will i be there
    or in some darker haven?

    Someone tell me where i am and when to get off,
i muttered in that tunneling grave
and my fellow dead cursed me.

    OK, i answered, *maybe i'm not in this after all.*
I'm in Newark or maybe in Baltimore or in Boston.
But, people are still glaring at me. I'm of the wrong race,
i plan to mug them / steal their jobs / refuse them jobs
    which i'm hoarding for my least qualified third cousins.

What are we dying of? some sort of jangle
If you ask *did we get off yet,* i don't think we can.

[1]Manhattan Schist, a black rock, is the bedrock of Manhattan.

WEST COAST MÉRINGUE

IT was the morning of the Great Rat Race, o rejoice in the new day.
We all foamed up out of the cracks and made a dash for the
                                    mortgage line.
It was the split levels against the ranch houses, flood tide out of
                                    sorts with points,
        all teeth / sharp, furry snouts / pointy ears twitching
        taste of salt / whiskery glints / ripples in the red dawn,
and with us the day's exchange rates, the red gold on our backs.

I dreamed I balanced on a surfboard in my Matronform Scar
and all the swimming pools in L.A. grew together
        connected by one long corridor of current event slosh.
Turning our backs on the East, we roared up out of San Diego Bay
                in one scalloped, humpbacked wave,
                    swishtailed North,
                whooped through Beverly Hills, rippled, slalomed
                    right up through L.A. into the Dos Sombreros
                        Real Mixican Restaurant
                    which was joined to all other restaurants by the
                                    same ceramic corridor.
I swam onto the floor, slithered across
flat
    belly to tiles
                under the tables
                        between the platform shoes
                        and the cowboy boots
under the rungs of chairs
                    overhung by the farslung rumps of guava jelly eaters.

What freedom on terracotta tile to squirm and slide
those leveraged buy-outs all the way to San Francisco
yea, even unto Berkeley, unto Oakland and the fiery gates of steel.

Jérôme, Jérôme Bosch, my kindly light:
We are all swimming in each other
                in that sweet
                        gold
                            heat.

SURROUNDED BY JERKS

South Africa and elsewhere

> "God send every gentleman. . .
>   Such hawks, such hounds, and such a leman. . ."
>   —old ballad

Gᴏᴛ a bird here. I'm going to break its wing.
Thing's small now. When it grows let's hope it can sing.
It'll have to work for its keep if it can't fly.
It's a nasty brute, though. Tried to peck out my eye.
Guess it's no songbird. Some vulture, some damn big king
killer crow. Got rhythm all right (but it still won't sing.
On purpose!)

Got a dog here. Think I'll knock in its head.
Make it mind what I say. Seems to want to bite instead.
Dog with a broken head has got no mind
to speak of, can't tell its head from its behind.
Too dumb to fetch or roll over. Kick it back into its bed.
Bet it's learned its place now (too bad the filthy beast is dead.
On purpose!)

Got a two-legged mother here, got to cut out its heart.
Treat 'em rough, you know they like it. Can't let them fart
around. If they can't carry on or cut up you can plug them in,
hook them up, get a free massage, push a button to begin.
Trouble is, some of these mean bitches are born smart-
assed: you can't work them round the clock (they just fall apart.
On purpose!)

Things are just no good anymore. My dumb bird won't fly
or sing, my damn dog won't bark, wag its tail, or lie
down, lick my feet when I need that. Some dead thing's crawled
                                        under the bed, lurks
there, baring its teeth. Lazy shits don't know the meaning of work.
I'm surrounded by jerks and kaffirs. They've kicked the world to hell.
If we burn it will be their fault (and what's more, they smell.
On purpose!)

THE PRINCE OF GARSTADT-PFLÜMË

> "The King beneath the Mountain
> The King of carven stone,
> The lord of silver fountains
> Shall come into his own!"
> —J. R. R. Tolkien, *The Hobbit*

THE Prince of Garstadt-Pflümë
is come into his own
his hands can measure spoonbowls
his country is not known

Upon the wrecks of caskets
his lazy fingers play
like light upon a tractor
rusting into day

His heart shall find no haven
between navel and crown
the Prince of Mumstadt-Pflèghmë
whose nose is falling down

How shall his minions tally
the onions millions pay
for mullions skullions carry
when scallions fly away?

He's riding hell for leather
down all the roads you own
the Prince of Schmierheim-Pfooey
whose belly-button's flown.

PART TWO: GRAND MAJESTIC STOMP

"Time held us green and dying . . ."
—Dylan Thomas, "Fern Hill"

THE ICE LIZARD: *CARNIVALE!*

*L*ADY, *why are you crying?* i asked her.
I want you to change me, she croaked.
Are you mine then? i asked. *Did i make you?*
I'm the world's, she answered. *You woke me....*

It was carnival time / she had on miles
of ice white satin with sequins, cut a fine figure.
A little nightmusic, please, she croaked, winking
a jeweled eyelid. *It gets too quiet down here
under the house. I don't get much action.
Break out your blue kazoo.* Well, i played
"Mam–mee, how I love ya;" she didn't move. I played
a slow, smoky blues; she hated it. I obliged
with a boogie. The sharp sail on her back sprang up
then   she shook it
                    WHOOPEE!
  The ice light of her eyes flickered, reflected
from the stone walls. The ice smoke of her breath shivered
the stone air. The ice knives of her
spine cracked the stone room. Her three hundred carat
squarecut vulgar diamonds flashed
over acres of scales. She sashayed. She shook.
She pawed the ground. She tossed her head.
She swelled. She filled out. She filled the room.
Her green / smoking / muscled flanks flung me
backwards through the door / flattened me
against the basement wall. With the roar of a glacier cracking
seedlings of itself through the stiffened lips
of a bay into frozen seas, she heaved her broad tail
out of the ice age caves, and rampaged up
      through the cellar ceiling
        the house
            through windows doors   chimneys.

Each green glass shard
each brass hinge and handle
joined itself to her scales, moved with her like a rhinestoned
showpiece, grew to her shimmy / each city
window sent its teeth to her strut
each house shook / rained itself onto her scales
bricks / tiles, magnetized / snapped to her skin
and stomped / stomped / WHOOPEE TIME!
                In the whole city
not one structure remained that was not / all over her. Naturally,
everything fell with her when she
     with no warning at all
          tumbled down in a heap
to rest.

When i woke under her body, that pile of rubble
into which i had snuggled as it coiled its domed, sheltering temple
over me, i looked up at her vaulted neck,
her proud, distant face
towering / older than memory / eyelids closed.
From their edges / through gullied cheeks / i saw the glacier
tears coil down: *I dance with the world,* she said.
                Make me a new one.
     I want you to make me a world where I can whoop it up a little
                without knocking the house down.
     I want life to shimmy and stomp with me and not fall apart.
     Make me something exuberant, something generous, something
                big enough to hold me, something that will
                     curl and arch as my neck arches,
                     that will shelter multitudes,
                that will rise up as my head rises up
                to raise you with it,
                that will love you
                     as my eyes and my tongue and my miles of jeweled
     skin love and love. I want to live in a world fit for love.
     Make me a world, she said. *Make me a world.*

WHOOPEE
(a round)

We had
nothing to work with, we said
all that we had to, we had
luck for all seasons, we said
nothing worth saying, we did
everything foolish, we said
everything needed, we had
time for a killing, we did
time in the shower, we called
all of our friends up, we had
ham and potatoes, we called
ghosts from the darkness, we told
all of our friends off, we held
hands in the darkness, we said
all that we thought of, we held
out when we had to, we told
lies in the darkness, we had
sex in a nutshell, we made
something of nothing, we had
something worth saving, we made
whoopee   /   all year round.

MARGUERITE'S SPINNING SONG

Wʜᴇɴ the long day lies down to farm
the night, look how i make my dawn
swim up the stream my dark rides on,
leap up the falls my life pulls down.

All night i make my day cry *done,*
all day i make my dark leap high.
Black of dream flares my morning sky,
red sun cools down my veins' deep run.

Let go, quick, momma, on the run:
from seed to runoff, cliff to kyll,
meltwater hands to gullied hill,
from hawk's deep plunge to tide's light comb.

Let go, split, momma, round the rim:
i set each counterweight you spill,
i swing the sun up as you spin,
you are the thread and i the will

from eyes to hollowed veils of skull
to that deep well your mind must fill.

THE IMMORTALITY OF THE HOTROD

I was soldered together from any old junk
by a farmboy who raided the lots for scrap, and i stood
in the courtyard, shaking and blowing, forty days
before he quit me. Some spark he lacked skill
or heart to breathe into me left me dead at the post
with all my thundering horsepowers frozen within me.

Drumtap / rains / rusted my dashboard to salts
lovingly polished that soughed in my stained buckets.
My stickshift plunged through the floor, then left off ploughing.
One fender was stolen to patch a pocked old barrow
whose wheels croaked high and low their rasp of praise.

Still, in the foam-specked starlight, nights when clouds
fingered counterpoints on the instrument board of the moon,
thrashing, boy and girl played at dibbles my mold-deep chassis,
knees bent, heaved, buttocks jouncing,
as my spent engine rode and drove them home.

SONNET OF THE RAIN

I shall speak of the rain for it has a long awakening
it rises out of the earth in its heavy steam
it cooks from the soil dank breath of swelling things
it sticks to my skin outdoors and won't come clean.

It coils through my hair with the cool sleekness of worms
twining / raises its heads / to fix you in stone.
When you look it cries: how shall i rise, how shall i turn
fever, pestilence, cold shakes to the gold scaled foam

of these seas that break on your soul in a tongue's flame?
Cries out: how shall i ripen? how shall i make you whole
unless the sun call me? how shall my fall slake
your thirst? Dear you / my earth / my opposite / fold

home harbor of all my desire, how shall i cover you,
lave you and make you new / as now i do?

FOREIGN EXCHANGE BLUES

"Bald sinkt das Schiff zu Grund, das Meer geht drüber
Und die versunken sind, sucht nur der Hai im See
Da hilft kein whisky mehr und kein 'Henry Clay . . .' "★
—"Matrosen-Tango," Berthold Brecht

WELL, i am not 'henry clay,' am not
tobacco, now think, think again
how many things i am not, not
poor woodrow wilson half his body
and mind dead with stroke, forgive
the multitudes i'm not for you;
i'd like to be them all, be ropes
of seaweed drying over pearls,
be onion bagels fresh and hot,
be cream cheese, be new herring when
they run and are not salted, be
a clotted line painted one night
by jackson pollock round your not yet
ready eyes, be chess, be well-spiced
bloody marys on the rocks, be
the pound, the deutschmark, the swiss franc,
the yuan, the yen, all acting right,
strip off the things i am and throw
a party made of sass and fight,
but i am not those things tonight.

★Soon the ship goes down, the sea goes over,
  and the sunken will be sought only by the shark in the sea
  no whiskey will help ever again, and no 'Henry Clay . . .'

BEACHCOMBING

        meaninglessly
your voice in the night
        washes back to me
           as if i had let myself go
        in a far sea
with the drift of your hands
        under the reefs
           trailing away
              in the loosening cold
           under the long
              curving strokes
        of the falling free
foam-written, shell-flecked line
        on the broken scree
tongue of rock, tongue of tide,
        tongue of weed, memory
           tossed up here again
              to swallow your name

FABLE OF THE DATE TREES

Don't pull down the shade. I'm back in last summer's breeze
where i've always been. There was never any heat but this
since the world began. There was never any desert night
but this one that drifts with the dunes as we feel our way
till the stars cut out. There was never any sleep but yours.

I won't forget what the light was like. I won't forget
that the sands were never certain we'd found the way
and the stars wouldn't tell us, the mistral forgot to say . . .
the date trees that shaded us might have been water dreams.
Even now i am never certain, i am never at ease.

BALLADE OF THE GRINDSTONES

"In the dark all cats are grey."
　　—old proverb

"In the dark they are all the same."
　　—Petruchio, in Cole Porter's
　　　"I've Come to Wive it Wealthily in Padua"

W HEN you and i draw close at night and play
those individual tricks all love keeps by,
do you believe i see you or can say
which hand beats mine, or by what bones i lie?
Thrown down by dark, who separates the high
from the low play? What flow of skill can claim
to tell by taste the mouth that drinks it dry
that night which makes us all lie down the same?

You ride the dark, but can you choose the bay
from the dark horse, or by your wits descry
which cat howled, at that hour when all are grey,
or what bitch held and wrung you, by her cry?
Lift up our bodies, raptors, we will fly,
circle and soar and, held each one by name,
drop, but all holds are equal when we pry
that night which makes us all lie down the same.

A tremor and a flash cry holiday
and these husks leap. Now tell me can we try
by touch which millstones grind our grain away
or whether in that press we love or die?
When the fine fever twists our straight awry,
rakes off our soft particulars, how blame,
each one, the other's harsh, unseeing eye,
that night which makes us all lie down the same?

After those teeth have gripped me by the thigh
and made my flesh and yours shake with one flame
shall either know which fire is you, which i,
that night which makes us all lie down the same?

A SLOW MEASURE

U NDER the homing current hunger ranges
under sea / such unseasonable changes
what the gull drops the crab's claw rearranges

The gulls call out what the new day reveals
oceans reborn in glow of orange peels
what the gull drops the crab's claw rearranges

What fact will have my dear and earth turn over
the winds wash clean and tides in time recover
undersea turns unseasonable / changes

Rock rises out of dust / what dawn wears down
with call of gull and crack of claw the town
returns us in the night the times will drown

undersea / what unseasonable changes
under the homing currents
                          what love ranges

MIRANDA'S BIRTHSPELL

1

In a redwalled cave, tied down
on a frame, hard pressed, pressing hard to get you out,
in pain and afraid of pain, protected from unclean
hands and all ills but pain and the fear of pain,
my heart pumps blood for you and i promise you again:
tomorrow i'll hold an ear of corn over your head till your
                                        thoughts leap
like a field in flower, make you suck sugar till your words run sweet;
you'll take honey in your hands and happiness will stick to your palm;
you'll suffer no want, for i'll go buy you dimestore pearls,
so you can fling jewels in the gutter as if born to worlds of wealth.

        In the redwalled cave
        where i count the dangers that cradle you, i am not myself.
        I am one with all women in bloodprint and birthpit who
                                        twisted
        good spells, bad spells, and waited for their blood to run free.
        in that space before mind, my mind is not my mind
        but the mind of an animal / outside all known rule.
Tomorrow i'll rub your fingers with roasted spiders
so those fine ashes will run nimbly over music and human hearts;
skin of sleek snake will slide over your skin so lightly
that anyone who tries to hold you will find you've slipped through.
Hair of hornless beast will blend with your hair so easily
that you shall shake off all hunters.

        In the redwalled cave
        where i crouch with you in a task of tearing, i see
        time beads the eyes of waiting dangers brighter than teeth
                                        to a kill

knits up the knucklejoints, knots in a noose for you to tell;
the water breaks hot on my thighs and i count my tears.
Remember always, what was one thing can never break. You are
trapped in me,
bound to me forever, as i to my mother, by a cord of force
which thins to invisible but pulls like the sun.
I bear witness my body continues to feel with the flesh i lose:
my unknown life, my parasite which has swollen my blood,
my child, my secret light that will out, my strength, when you bleed
some fourteen years from now in another world, this stay-at-
home blood
in this body, this cave, this cell, this emptying self
shall feel that pull, and clot to an unseen wound.

2
How shall i keep you safe once i let you go?
I must learn to protect my blood, when you wake to smooth
your shape from the sheets, when you walk to sweep out your prints
so no enemy can plant stone to bruise, glass to cut,
when you pierce hand or foot with a nail to scrub that nail
every day until your wound heals and infection dies,
starved of your blood on its iron. I must teach you a wisdom i lack:
to choose your pain, to be hurt by no unclean thing.
What wisdom can hold such a tumble? Confined
in this redveined cell, locked up in my life
with you locked in me and forcing your passage out,
i twist with you in our pain, i shout aloud
to the predators where they wait, as the blood spouts
from the womb which must shield you and drop you and
has no choice:
the blood and the tears are the life / no way out of that tide.

But to let you fall to your death? No, sooner, tomorrow
shall i shake a potlid over your closed eyes
till the drops condensed there wet your cheeks and cheat time,
and your tears, unlike mine, are spent young?—before nightfall, toil

after each trace you scatter, child prodigal
of shed clothes, teeth, hair, nails, print of foot and body?
What a Mother's Day of pains i should celebrate then
picking up after you: your hale life's trail:
leavings of food, one flesh with the food you have eaten,
the point that pierces you polished, the cord underground,
no shred left! Unmarked, leaving no mark,
you would push through these straits a frozen stream,
delivered
from blood in blood and still not free of our blood.

I bear witness your body must feel with the flesh you lose:
though the hairs on your head be numbered, those you must sow
on comb, on pillow, or with your life leap up to witness you,
not veil, not helmet, eclipse, but unseen corona.
In this sudden foam
the mill of your nine months' turning under my heartbeat
grinds out still, as the falls pull the stream through the millrace
birth after birth in gouts that clot and shake free
as the hollow womb shrinks / keeps the print of fullness.

3

This, then, is the labor, the hard act of birth:
not to push you out of this cave or out of this body
but to get you out of myself, my love's strength,
my fear which stops the channel against all life
in the name of safety and motherhood and love,
push you out of all shelter, riding our common bloodtide
into enemy hands. Your head has just sliced through me.
I must let you slide out in the exile that fills our morning.
This hard air cuts us both.
Dear, almost born,
bruised with your fight to elbow your passage through me,
i bear witness our bodies must feel with the flesh we lose.
Measure: the blood i pump out now with you
is more than can fill my body. Let me drop all fear for you

with a calm pressure of strength, as my voice shouts now
and the birth yell, resonant, fills this room between shouts,
as our cut hair will guard our heads in a radiance of force,
as our cast nails will mark deep, as our blood when it clots
still links the wound to the flow.

        In this redwalled room
        where together we strain towards breath, as we shall in
                                      our time
        strain away from each other, the sponge from the cord,
                                   and not break,
        in this hollow hold in ourselves where the predators wait
        sure in a foretaste of blood, where you swim and climb
        and wrestle my flesh away, bear witness now
how we cast away our lifeline in making this birth
and the line still holds, how surely you ride out the tide,
how you make the air yours with your welcome, triumphant cry,
how the tears that were mine are yours and hold us fast,
you who are mine and not mine and my daughter at last.

THE END OF LOVE
(for Alison)

A_s
the time when i shall not
move
    anymore
        moves
quietly
    within these words

as you, my daughter
moved
    quietly
        in your turn
within me
    and i listened
        one hand fitted
like the ear
    of a blind woman
to the belled vault you rode,
the swell, the turning
    outward
to the free
    unknowable
transparency
    you would breathe

so the end
    of love
        moves
quietly
    in these words
draws me where it draws
me, one breath

after
another, outward, each
in its turn
without touch
without intention

so pulls me
out of myself
with you
to let go
in the free
unknowable
sea that breathes us
to make
still
such ease as lies
in our nature

HOLDING THE BRIDGE

Do you remember the old days, when i said, *i've been far away,*
and you, thinking of your last trip, guessed i meant, maybe, California?
I couldn't, facing your silence, that flash between one of us coming
back, one of us leaving, tell you all of it, flat.
It hadn't been California, no place that near.

It was as if i'd stood on a bridge, facing death,
   holding back the Goths and the Vandals,
      saving what was to be saved
         loving what was to be loved
           knowing it would do no good
   seeing clearly that what we'd loved would go up in flames
   the huge wave come, the quake plough cities under,
   our children be enslaved, thrust down to rage
      in impotent darkness, all knowledge lost
         the ground wasted, eaten
           with salt, the face of love changed from itself
  you changed, dishonored / my life stained for nothing
and still i'd fought on there / to hold off that flood for a moment.

Oh You, long gone, not California, no place that far
Right here i've stood on the bridge, mad as Canute
   doing the dishes / running the laundry / packing
   school lunches / paying off debts as they came due
      telling the truth when i could
         lies when i had to
and though i couldn't hold back that tide
   and your face changed from itself
      became the barbarian horde
         though the last we knew of honor
     and love most shamefully
         went under
i don't regret that long defeat.

With my good will, my work   /   i held death off while i could.
It was worth all it cost, though i died for it,
there, on the bridge.

PART THREE: THE VIGIL

"Pay attention to what they tell you to forget..."
—Muriel Rukeyser, "Double Ode"

THE ICE LIZARD'S VIGIL

In that clarity which comes of having let things
go, i went downstairs to the sub-basement
where she i could not bear to remember lay
frozen in her ice age. Against the seamed walls
leaned things i had forgotten: old sneakers,
broken necklaces, torn curtains, ice skates,
hockey sticks, rifles, machetes, my four years dead
Bialy-cat's red collar.

At the limestone room's back wall
she coiled, grown into the rock, her huge tail
looped down into the earth's dark
center   head bowed
claws covering her eyelids
from which the sluggish, green
glaciers crawled.

Do you need me again? she croaked. *I thought you'd forgotten me.*
I need you, i said. *Though the whole house stands between us,*
beams, ceilings, floors, rugs, skulls, when the middenheap
is too much with me i come back to you.

No, she said, blinking her cold, crusted eyes.
I remember what lies behind time. You have used me endlessly.
Whatever happened to generosity? Does nobody at your end
of history remember what I need?

A GRIEF BEYOND REMEDY

ONCE again the machine breaks down. She kicks it twice.
No go. / Her mother stands over it, glaring
as if it were just one more unhandy daughter
she loves but can't live with. If only machines could listen.
It's all someone's fault. The damn thing wasn't brought up right,
was indulged or treated too strictly, not tenderly nurtured,
not taught to succeed. Someone blew out its motor
by overload, or left the front window open
till it sputtered and coughed and came down with the flu.

Once again the grown daughter is there in her mother's house,
a small child, helpless. Every morning she drags downstairs
to the doctor's prescribed menu that makes her gag.
She sulks and loses weight, nobody knows why.
Each day the stream of "suggestions" breaks surface at dawn,
forcing her downriver.
                    Green is not her color.
    She should cut her hair short so people won't see that it's oily.
    She should put on a dress; jeans are for the country
    and the uncouth. Her homework is carelessly copied
        (appalled, she hears herself tell her young daughter this)
    her children ill-taught, her husband not kept in order
        (will she tell her daughter this too, ten years into the future?)
    her career tossed aside, her life put together stupidly,
    her furniture undusted, the wrong style, and badly arranged.
        (Is there no help for it, will all these things be true
        of her young child, as they may be true of her?
        when she speaks to her daughter, will her voice sound like this?)
    Not one of her daily machines to insure survival
    can work. She should send them to the Thrift Shop and copy her mother's.

She is not alone. There is nobody alive
or dead whose life her mother couldn't have planned and run better,
whose happiness her mother wouldn't have made good and sure of
had they all done everything other than what they did:

She knows it, this strong woman
who has worked for her family all her stubborn life,
who stood behind her husband like a rock that knew better,
upon whom all his work must constantly be beaten back
to run aground, to be shattered into wreckage, and then rebuilt
and sent out to sail, this time her own chosen craft,
her device, her machine, her ship, seaworthy and sure:

this strong woman
who tossed her own talent out for the laundry, the dishes,
the crafting of her children's minds, the tending of their talents,
the typing of her husband's letters, the work of keeping
the whole raft afloat as if they would sink without her,
as if they would even now, every single one,
sink to the bottom if she dared to let them alone:

this woman who drives them crazy and whom in the wreckage
                they treat with forbearance,
as her young daughter forbears her now, in grief and anger,
as her mother forbears her now, in love and terror
                as of a mirror
each time they touch
                each time they touch.

BODY POLITIC

You think yourself Aeneas, it may be,
and call me Dido: easy to leave. You claim
i hold you with intolerable demands,
say i fast net you whom your gods force free
and fire upon the planet to found Rome,
your Pax Romana bleeding from your hands.
I am no Dido though i am your home,
your vault which, once you join me, justly stands
communitas, the city's network. See:
that room, that arched chain, that linked self, that dome
you'd raise, i am. Not elsewhere. Here. Demands
your flame an honest peace built honestly?
Turn from mine, all Rome's roads will take false turns.
The Pax Humana burns as my hearth burns.

IN JANE'S RED ROOM

Someone is painting red floors, someone is shaking
the brush so it splatters raised dots in the wet gunk.
Someone is drinking, crying, staggering, aching,
cries like a blooded paintbrush / rockdancing drunk.
Curses spatter the walls with dried / paint,
curses fall on the floor from the bleeding walls,
the curse bleeds off the walls. Some vampire saint
lets the life soak into each sheet as the life falls.
Raised dots strike one on another, pimples, hives:
scratch and they flake days off in itching scales.
Moment and moment itches: the ringworm lives
pattern the night: minds behind drops, spots, rails
in their cowering beds, the floors that hold them up,
the red plague under their feet when at last they drop.

TAKING STOCK

How shall you love me? If i come
in prudence and maybe a margin of pride
to count the ways, be deaf and dumb.
Keep no tally, take no advice,
let nothing of interest build, don't sign
any notes. When our term's up and all's done
pretend an ignorance clear as ice
and reckon nothing i tell you to.

If we tax ourselves, as redlines crumble,
to stagger into a closing, wise
as brokers when all stocks fall / let's plunge;
all killings are stumbled upon. Call us sly
bankers of life: market-letter and science
may guide our investments, not the crude
luck of the gambler. (But when foresight dies,
take count of nothing i tell you to.)

If tomorrow you try the stockpage to study
my curves and read out odds, think twice.
How many who came with a wintry judgment,
reckoning only their single sight,
played blind and justly lost. If tonight
the hand you hold doesn't measure true,
consider that measure and justice lie,
and balance nothing i tell you to.

Client, how shall we end? If ever i light
the way, be sure no gains will accrue.
Close out all holdings, like justice, keep blind;
hold tight to nothing i tell you to.

THE ART OF CONVERSATION

*T*oo late, i said, and threw my plate at his ear.
The world dished out too much this time. I won't
play. No more give and take for me.
I'm not here.

No good, he swore, and stuck his fork in my brain.
Coming and going, this time, old bitch, you went
too far. Even if your door were open, i'd rather stay
out in the rain.

All quiet, i wrote my sisters when the fur
stopped flying. *We're about even. I kept count.*
But he's hung out in the woodshed all week. This way
we'll go real far.

WUZZIT

(a counting out rhyme)

Going home from your house the night
bent and i lost you, *goodbye house,*
i took the train back, *goodbye train,*
i took the night back, *goodbye night,*
i took the wrong bent back and i

counting one two, *counting one,* bent
took two, took the wrong train back, all the
counting one two, *one way,* took the wrong one
back two, *all one,* counting one two, count
the wrong night, it went back, i took
counting wrong the house, *one back,* two counting

bent, i took the wrong you back here, *goodbye*
house, goodbye train, goodbye night, bent,
goodbye you, good by you, one two,
i took the wrong good by here, *one bent,*
here *two,* i am not counting you.

STEENWEG

S TONEROAD
            highway.
Nobody talk to me, i'm all through
with answering. The cobblestones
which last summer ate through
my shoes tramping them made
more of an answer. Now
they're under snow.

        Who's got
the sun, who's got the death car
to take me over?
                  Not
    any sun, not any snowfall:
    a neutral substance, rocksalt
    might do. I'd better get
    what's like me, inert
    in itself, becoming a largesse
    only through contact, irritants scattered to fret
    the mood i dropped last night
    over all of you.

            See, it's drilled
through, pocked, puckered, cratered, raveled,
lace now, a patchwork of foolish
embroidery over the roadstones
which / like / rocksalt
do nothing, wait underfoot
to be known. Black, clumped,
angry, they chew up the sheet
that covered them. Well, they're
hard, won't easily yield but
we can go miles on
them. They can take weight.

WHAT THE ROADBED KNOWS

W HEELS gliding over my eyes, over my hair
night sliding, smooth as wheels in a quiet place
I was here, I was there, I am not yours

water that combs the houses between their bricks
water that whispers over rooftop and sill
I was here, I was there, I am not yours

in the quickness of secrets when just one night slips by
water under the lips, under the eyelids
wheels gliding over my eyes, over my hair

fingers that search out silence from airscoop hollows
whirlwind drilling the cheeks, saltgrain, sandwhisper
I was here, I was there, I am not yours

mouth of horizons, parched mouth of the sunset desert
cascade, crumbling earth gulf, rockslide and gulley
wheels gliding over my eyes, over my hair

floodwater roll covering body and tongue
fire swirl / roar / blaze of the giant wind
wheels gliding over my eyes, over my hair
I was here, I was there, I am not yours

SOME FAR PLACE

(a counting out rhyme)

You have come from some far place
you are going to some far place
alone when you wake you will remember
to take your hat and go alone

until you arrive at some far place
in stone. You are leaving tomorrow late
you will always leave tomorrow late
when you get here you will remember

to take your hat and go out there
to wait. You have been here before me
you will never forget / how to be here
before me. Tomorrow when things come clear

you will remember to take your hat
right here in stone you will not wait
you will keep on going to some far place
alone. alone. alone. alone. alone.

ENTERING DAY

Love ran fast
                you fell away
                        all far long
the foundations of that house wouldn't hold sand out.
The wolves lay down. Now, after the chase was done
you saw their tongues
                    red the dark.

Tell the house to pull back from the tangled rock
the earth to stop shaking.
                      What fire or lie-down earth
can make you quiet? The sun sometimes lies down
to the taste of anger. You're going to let go too.

Like one who climbs winter
like the sun pushing past the clouds / entering day
like the hiss and slice of a blade that whites the water
love will fall away and you'll lie down free.

THE IRON MUSE

A morning came when he could wake, his face
sleep damp against my shoulder, and not wake.
He could inhale that first deep breath you take
knowing you live
        and not wake to my skin.

Unkindled we wait
        breathe out, breathe in
breathe in below-zero air, breathe out banked fire;
in: lethargy; out, out: blow out desire;
in: broken glass, changed locks; out: that perfume
which, in a fine suspension, atomized,
perfused the gentle fevers love inspired
into his skin and mine; breathe in the way
alone, as embers scatter, their flames expire;
breathe out the last iced night, the silent room
and clock that could not give the little death
we found once in each other; breathe out the great,
the clanking, iron death, the gulf-eyed death,
back to back, staring; breathe: *the weight, the weight;*
breathe out: *wake, wake;*
        breathe in: *my love, too late.*

SNOW ON A MOONLESS NIGHT

Washington Park, Albany

Moon, my empty gong / sound of this snowfilled night,
you've spun on this fraying string more than ten years,
seen that the one you loved
so long was a hollow shape holding hard
to its heart a selfish child soul. Give it up.

    Not that he deceived you but that you deceived yourself
    not that he betrayed you but that you betrayed yourself
    not that he devoured you but that you devoured yourself
    that in your changing / you failed to change.

Black amphora in shards on a marble floor,
since that round belly can't swell
again around its own fragments, there's no help
you must let the splinters   /   speak for the whole.
—

Old powdered disc, dust ghost
those huge forms
you saw once: how shall you know the forms of life,
the compass whole? Alone at your stand late night
look out at the crusted park, snow leaching the ground
try to measure yourself by what you can contain:
    you were an idiot   you loved a balloon
    a mockman, a Tartuffe.
    Your children took root in lies. Where's their true ground?
    All moonshine.

Look out at the trees, their trunks, their knotted roots
you are yourself the thing you would contain.
—

Sliver moon, shadow-mirror
what's left? How can you take your own distance?

There's a night when even moons crawl into a hole.
You've known, like the Moor of Venice, your own dark
when that globe you held the model of truth
turned from candid map to false projection
no clean white lawn to die in but blank Sahara
all latitude and no honor. Surrounded by lies
not even the Moor's last comfort / to know it all lies:
this was true.

Can you wash that night clean again with your charity
before the pity of it winks you out?
—
Needle moon, sickle arms hugging a whisper
ghost in the snowfilled night,
how you watch the squirreltail dance of the shadow trees
which once you lit, pregnant after all with yourself /
how you hug your self to your heart / hear it cry
for light from a dry breast. Give it this truth, then,
that lies curled in your globe, an unborn dwarf:
that was your unlived life. You died of it.

                        Drained bag, old closed eyelid,
shrunken to fit a sandhole socket,
now on the moonless, unlit snow, look out
without sight, see how the snow wakes its own light.

PART FOUR: WHAT THE RAIN TAKES

"Atteste quelque cigare . . .
Que la cendre se sépare
De son clair baiser de feu . . ."

—Stéphane Mallarmé, "Toute l'Âme Résumée"

As some cigar might swear . . .
That the ash severs itself
From its clear kiss of fire . . .

CANTICLE OF THE FOREIGN WARS

Take up this instrument and tell me what feels foreign
in its heft or its neck's curve.
Have the tautnesses of its cords
slackened
    learned to jar?
Where are those harmonics your ear expects with familiar chords?

When the children were starving in the Khmer passes, and under
                                        foreign
stars their eyes echoed against the night,
and their voices drowned all art,
you asked me what news of the far front: why were we not there
to resolve the fugues of need to one whole, tonic chord.

What word could i carry of these children, no more foreign
now their first subject rang clear
and they put hunger on   /   as if taking off a mute?
How many died before we learned to sort
their cadences from the rumor of all other chords?

Here every voice sounds distant as a boat, foreign
to hope, its cargo wracked by fever, exile, war,
cast up on surf, on rocks, then forced out once more,
cracked, oars creaking off key, compass overboard or off true,
                                        sails torn, nets torn,
water and food gone, cast off, forgetting shore.

Do you think if we were there the mere force of that foreign
agony would winch our voices back on true
which now untuned from our neighbors croak in the dark?
Don't make us witness of the power of art, of love, to trivialize.
How should we join the world, who play our loss

of ourselves like a lute, or how should that world tune us, being foreign
to our discords, to that clear, single cry which makes the earth
                                    one chord?
In that sound we resound, but this is no canticle of the power of
                            art, of love, to redeem;
nor does that croaking wreck sound out its singular note
to make hum the daily thoroughbass of our loss.

We touch what we can; our bodies grow more foreign.
Back set against back, leaning hard on each other, enemy and support,
we send out our divorce away from each other across the
                            resonant world,
witness of the power of art, of love, to restore
nothing, though it give voice to good and evil and the world's loss.

Friend, lover, my brother and enemy, i cannot mend us in these foreign
wars, as we drive blindly for opposite ports.
I know that your voice and mine once were single as a white roar
of steady light, that now are separate and winking as two stars,
that wink, and wink, and still we light no shore.

64

Before Notre Dame:
(for my mother's eightieth birthday and my father's eighty-fourth)

WHAT THE RAIN TAKES

WHAT the rain takes
                    it will give back to you
as these bronze statues of saints
                    on the Cathedral roof
dissolve their glow

Those years you used what you knew
            to carve out my eyes, chipped sharp
                    at the corners to hold this pen,
channel where tears have run

those statue years
when angry and grieved
            you watched my mind lie
            in a dying marriage
and dared not speak
            my voice, your work,
            wasted, turned
                    from its promise
                            angry at you
                    whose silence,
                                    nonetheless,
                    spoke

Even so, as it washes the years,
            the earth will mend us
                    wash your minds and mine
from sombre bronze
            to its own clear
                    green

MARCHERS OF RAGNAROK

One: BIFROST

WHY, friends, what passage is this, why do we wake
all the stones of the night with our stiff tread? I have rung
like those stones with your footfall. There is no way you can take
up that steep arch and not hammer my skull like a gong.

See those tall steps of night stand clear while all known
stars limn their edges. These very suns round whom
no worlds swing, and these, whose unpredictable worlds have grown
deadly crystals, cement tight the steps we make our doom.

Ancient night: unable to hear anything but the night / steel
and brass, speaking terribly out of their centuries' dream,
how much night will we need to wake, how much forging to yield
the last flint of ourselves to this stockpiled boneyard? See

how we cleave to ourselves, the night gouging steps from your still
eyesockets, the watchfires summoning night from my skull.

MARCHERS OF RAGNAROK

Two: THE SPOILERS AND THE SPOILS

THE night too struggled to escape this pitted field.
The whole night long night waited for us to fail,
while all night's forces muttered in their retreat
and the fires poured over us, melting our shield wall.

The glue of our sinews melted, our joints rained
little meteors down, a hail of melting stones,
knucklebone, ankle and thigh. Though the field had been gained,
it gained nothing from us, and the marrow of our bones

ran clear in the turning currents of suns. When we woke,
the sound of the mortars gone, and the mortars of stars
melted, that joined those weightless blocks of black
eternal zero home to us, we fixed on, as hard,

neither our wills nor our fates. What we had taken
for our world was death without grief and all holds broken.

PERSPECTIVES

> ". . . Dear God, we pray
> To be restored to that purity of heart
> That sanctifies the shedding of blood."
>   —Robert Penn Warren, "Interjection #4: Bad Year, Bad
>   War: A New Year's Card, 1969"

FROM the night his mind pulls out an image. A figure
that gives nothing for touch and the world for line
stands by the wall to measure the universe
with its calipers. A thin string runs from his belly,
unseen, to a vanishing point. What can he see
in this city? An arched vista ticks off the background.

There, below, a man dies. In the middleground
the guts are uncoiled on a winch by a hooded figure.
The moon lies hooded. What can the artist see
in that curve? Do we scan the architecture, how each line
will bend our eyes to the gouged hole in the man's belly,
how the arches slant back to the edge of a universe

vanishing, to pull the whole weight of this universe
down to drill him and open him? Is he the ground
only, and color, the yawning mouth of the belly,
that splash, that hammering center, the true figure?
What shall we choose to touch in the corkscrew line
of those innards? Have we made or not made what we see

in perspective? Innocent of all but design, we see
head thrown back, chin thrust towards us to block out our universe
from those eyes, one knee up, one leg driving its line
straight from the wound to our eyes, the foot in the foreground
enormous and kicking. We have found an art to figure
alternates: not the wound but the reflex of pain, not the brilliant belly

68

flowering, but the extremity, the jolt. Let it belly
and crackle out in its innocence till we see
action, reaction, mesh, the one accurate figure
an artist of agony makes of our universe.
The slanted arches hurl us out from the foreground,
make us perspectives, force us to follow that line

till it turns on itself. Year after year we shall line
up, innocents, to look through the hole of that belly
into the opening pit where our mercies ground.
Under the moon's uncabling, the mind turns to see
the innocent with the calipers plot the universe
by how much his art can winch out of that figure.

He has figured it wrong. Can any cleanness of line
in a universe made to our measure fix that belly
with its guts in place when we see the guts paint the ground?

THE NORMAL

Buses have lifted the candy wrappers and matchbooks
to swirl in their wake / sucked down into the whirlpools,
the funnels, the swirling mouths of a city street.

All day in this wind i felt the force of the normal.
Under the long dull pull of wheels up this hill
i thought of the ordinary as if it were a green cloud
that could lean me to sleep under its gentle pressure.

Before Notre Dame:

IN LEAPING GREEN

In leaping green
            silent, when rain
on the roof
            melts us clean
                        my calm
saints, in your age
                i see you
outwait
        the long count
promises
        you might have kept
                        for yourselves
and made instead
            for me

I who was once
            your bronze
pride
    promise
            again
even as your love
            wrote me
even as wasted things
                remain
                    at rest
even as our skulls
            will filter out
the softness, the loss
            of eyes
leave only
        the hard parts

even as your fears for me
                    will fall away
and i
     come back to you

so time will mend us
                    under the sky
                                not make us worse
and everything you've given
                              though i change
i'll give you once more

REPORT ON THE EXPERIMENT "GALACTICHORE"
(Group 17A, The Green Blob From Outer Space)

F<small>ELLOW</small> Members of the Society,
we must tell you that the experiment
we prepared with adequate hope, performed with rigor,
was far from successful. The predicted results
did not follow. What occurred instead
left us with little prospect that any entity
can maintain its pure form
in the face of environmental bombardment.

We deposited our capsules, as agreed,
in various habitats: on planets circling binary stars,
white dwarfs, red giants, asteroid clusters, radio sources.
The encapsulated materials were at all stages of development:
atoms, molecules, crystals, minerals, spores,
one-celled animal life of purest clarity,
clusters of cells, differentiated, complexly grouped.
Those we had most hope for, the utterly pure,
unisouled, clear as the body of God whose great womb we are,
whole-minded, responding with instant, selfless intelligence
to each moment's push and tug,
those excellent, clean souls, visible thoughts,
those angels like unto which in time's loving gestation we pray
                                        to become
soon lost their integrity, devolved, broke down
into a questing duplicity, then ambition, thrusting,
separation of the soul-wall from the world, so that the self would not let
                        itself gently melt and flow
in that well of other selves who selflessly surround it.
From duplicity, then, to hunger, greed, endless questions,
to that questing which bespeaks the separation of the particle from
                                        the wave,
a perpetual twinning and increasing of one atomy at the cost of all,

73

minds divided, each soul individuated away from its sisters.
So these multi-souls formed systems and lost themselves,
broke down into swamps, nets, clusters, ganglions.
Not just one but all the units we deposited
devolved from atom to compound, spore to fungus,
cell to animal. . . .

Even when the animal world had grown itself
with such ingenuity as almost to redeem its primal loss
in a compensating extravagance of invention,
those fallen worlds continually repeated the first fall.
Each species, each kind, lost that which most made it whole:
the great dragon shrank, shredded scales to feathers, then shaggy fur;
the wolf rose up on malformed legs, compressed its wise muzzle
to flat snout, wrenched forepaws and tail to swing
in the trees; the ape it had so hideously become dropped to the ground,
forgot that noble crouch which had kept its eyes
and its brow close to the earth, its two hands low, full of grit,
reminding it of its excellent grub soul;
it stripped off the coat that had, like leaves or moss, kept it one
                                              with the weather,
stood naked, counted its losses, flayed its planet,
and so, in exuberant inventiveness / new-clothed itself.

All devolves
            naught holds. The primitive world soul,
we see, is unstable. The results of our study
lead us to propose the unthinkable: that, unhappily, we too
must be a step in the long falling off—
that even as cells, souls, radiant nodes of night
divide into vileness, so it must have befallen that once in the first heat
those pure atomies, particles, rays, God's instants in which Her
                                              world forms
and reforms, must also have lost themselves,
walled off, each from each, begun that seeking
collision from which our bodies / souls took shape.

We have not the heart to continue. In brief, we find ourselves
a midpoint in our Mother's endless loss,
Her breaking down from pure unity to corrupt multitude.
We see no hope that we can ever return
to Her single night which made us one glowing whole:
oh soul in which our minds take fire and die.

REPORT ON THE EXPERIMENT "ROMULUS 9"
(Observer #683, The Ape Mother Whose Cub Was "Special")

FELLOW Mothers of Wisdom, guardians of love,
i must tell you that the part of the experiment
i undertook at your behest
was not a success. There is no way we can redeem what we have
        become.

When the devolved female died in childbirth, and i informed you
that i had followed my milk's pull / suckled the cub,
you instructed me to continue, which i would have done anyway,
as you well knew, since it is not in us to abandon an infant,
however afflicted. I nurtured it in our traditions,
pitiful, flayed thing / fit its flat snout to my breast,
twined its bare claws in my coat, taught it to cling.
From my milk it learned not to kill needlessly, from my wrinkled
                                                        fingers
combing its sparse hair / not to indulge its hands
in manipulation, its mind in dominion / from my nostrils
sniffing at its throat, its belly, how touch creates love.

You had hoped to build a bridge in its brain between left and right,
between them and us, to hold that bridge, to reclaim the nerves,
to retrain the impulses in the old patterns,
re-evolve the cub back to that sisterhood from which it had fallen.
Maybe we might have succeeded had young Tarzan been female.
The data is insufficient; i will not generalize,
say biology is destiny. Maybe this human material is beyond grace,
has lost too much of its native tongue, palmpat, scent-touch,
gentleness of toe-hold, questing of muzzle,
has grown its brain too tall, too far from the ground
for the head to know what the earth and the heart are doing.

You know the outcome. Young Tarzan is no link—
not between sunlight and earthhome, not between mind and body,
not between us, my sisters,
and that beast we have become. I love him as self loves soul,
as i must love what i cradle. He loves me as servant,
harbor, fur, suckle, hollow / useful. He hates me
as if my embrace were quicksand and not nightcomfort.
I have heard that our cousins the wolves in the eastern tropic
have duplicated our experiment, with similar results—
young Mowgli is no link either. Only to the north
in Aveyron, the wolf mothers have had a partial success.
Their human child has retained an untracked brain,
early enough shaped to transcendence
that his people who have repossessed him could not destroy him;
unfortunately, if he is the bridge, they cannot use him.

It may be that our only hope to undo entropy
is for one of us to do fieldwork among them,
unsoul herself, go down
and speak to these creatures in the mire of their own symbols.
Certainly, i would not be prepared to make this sacrifice.
It is unclear at what stage the damage becomes permanent,
the lapse into abstract irreversible, the fieldworker forever
gone native, cut off from us, trapped in their patterns, losing her own.
The one who will endure this, falling into the light,
as i see one of us will,
must be bred for, generation after generation, to create sainthood,
to keep a form of sanity even after her redemptive fall.

But i see no hope of redeeming them or reversing our loss
though a thousand of our daughters fall in flames
like that first Lucy, carrier of light
(and this thought, i know, makes me a radical, a heretic, a mad thing
in your judgment). I do not believe that we are the ideal form
from which these naked savages have fallen. I think we ourselves
                                        have fallen
from some pure clarity at whose black radiance i can only guess.

Once the world's wholeness and beauty must have been ours.
We must once have been simple, sole, complete.
Out of my mother's heart, which has agonized
over my fallen human child, i bear witness to you:
we too were once God's perfect seed.
Hear me: the Lord our Mother, She is One;
we fell from Her dark, full, waiting emptiness into this world;
we were once that soul of love, that body of night.

POEM OF NEGATIVE DENSITY

WORDS like balloons, words like smoke, words like seeds:
these words are used so lightly, casually,
they float over my mind like dandelion puffs
into the changing fields. They will not stay
for study, they are too light to do hard labor.
They carry no freight. I can take any other words
in exchange for them and not come out the loser.
Look, your breath has blown them across the barrens.
Next year at this time a field will spring where they fell,
and all its sense be clouded saffron and silver.

After Cavafy:

THINGS OF THE HOUSE

SISTER, when one day after long thought you hold open that door
        through which the lost doesn't return
and you pace the hall back, don't blame yourself.
        You could never have been
what he goes to as eagerly as to his death.
Though the dust sheet shapes the livingroom couch
to his shape, though the chairs at dinner remember
        his thighs which bestrode their worlds
though the rims of glasses tell of his lips
still moving and how your pillow holds
        open his print, how your bed keeps
the hollow of his weight pressed down and touching you,
though your house and the things of your house knit
his shadow to yours like the shadows of wild disorder
after the party is over, though you live with these things
and in them through all your city's empty squares,
        let them drop like confetti.

Sister, when the day after long thought holds open the night's
body, and that far hollow of your self wakes
quietly into itself, float in with it slowly.
        You could never have held those tides
you swim in, though once you were all tides
and he all currents. Let the dust sheet
cradle that empty shape as it gathers
a self to itself, let the wine glass fill
        as the hollow of the light
pulls it around itself, let the dust motes lift
their dance into life, into that outline of fires,
that deep emptiness whose stars they hold and shape.
That space is your empire   /
                        hold it and rule.

80

After Cavafy:

THE PARTY AFTER ANTONY

THERE's a space which is yours, which you own now,
where the dance is over. What will you sweep away,
      what will you keep?

It was never your youth, that dry river, never thrones,
dominations, powers leaving, never your blood
you pushed out, never your better half, never your self.
(It was all you had to spill to make space wake.)
Get rid of the rings, butts, ashes, shards, dead ends.

          Sister, in that widening place,
with a whisper, a splash of flutes, with a drumming surf
caught syncopated   /   from another room,
with procession, with unvoiced eddies, with curls of triumph,
      with a breaking reverberation and foam,
as of a proud populace returning to its honor,
          not words but the hollows of words,
          not light but the ash of light,
          with a white, transparent dust
that dresses you in yourself, with the lightening of laughter
and glass   /   slivering far away in another house,
see how the nation you have become throws aside herself
          as befits a queen,
          how she stretches   /   yawns
reaches out carelessly to take that clear glass
seen only because it bends the light and repels the light
and contains the light, how she empties the light through her,
          how here in the space she owns
          her last dance begins,
how she holds the light up to the light and spills the light
          and wakes the night she bears.

RETURN OF THE ICE LIZARD

ON the third step from the top, i stood,
peering down into the old root cellar, in search of the Ice Lizard,
        she whom i had left there
            when i had no more strength. Near my foot
            lay a heap of ice skates and old
            shoulder pads, shin guards, armor
            from forgotten wars. The terminal moraine
            of the glacier had pushed them upstairs
            one foot per year.

She lay, half buried under frozen / paleolithic artifacts
in acres of steel grey satin, heavy with alexandrite and onyx.
Mother, i said to her. *Please wake up. I haven't forgotten you.*

Her yellow eyes opened. Steel lashes
hung stiff at their lower rims. *Do you need me again?* she croaked.

My love, i need you, i said. *Do you need me?*

Her eyes, bleak tundras
which had seen no thaw for all of time, stared at me.
I thought you'd never ask, she said. *I've never stopped waiting for you.*
What of our history: is it still in the rocks?
It's cracking too fast to read, i answered. *Now look*
                    what i've found for us to do.
I turned, and she turned after me, so carefully
as not to break off the glaciers she had grown
century by century out of her golden eyes.
I laced on my old ice skates, which still fit. I stepped out
onto the glacier's edge, balanced there
on its mirrored, creaking skin. *Look,* i said.
I can dance with you here. / Nothing will break
                    OUR ICE DANCE
                            Carefully, then

so as not to ring that ancient ice
awake too suddenly, i began to skate
            in gentle, arching curves. I wrote on her ice, slow
            swooping
                        exuberant
            flourishes / arabesques. I glided. I leapt.
            I twirled. I took off and returned in curlicues.
            As i swept into a wide
            turn, the ice light of her eyes glided
            with me, reflected the signature
            of my dance back to me, reflected her great sweep
            of light back to her from the stones. The walls,
            alive with the ice smoke of her breath,
strutted   pranced   bounded   the air
jiggled. She rippled. She cavorted. She glowed.
She swelled. She filled out. She filled the room.
There was no such thing as emptied
or used up where we were
                        Her frozen streams bore
            me up, my sharp blades wrote
            her life on her scales in
            streamers of light. Her neckridges
            jangled glass tendrils, filaments,
            icicle hair full of zip and jingle / her clawed feet
            strung ice cilia through the ceiling
            into the souls of stones, linked atom and atom.
With the sigh of a snow cloud sifting, drawing seedlings of its own
soft flakes through the winter air
            those green glass
            ice flows, those brown oak
            rockslides, those brass hinges and handles
            felt her scales join to them, melt them
            together like bootleg sap. No wall
between house and house / roof and sky / cell and self.
                        The city
clanked and jangled one charleston jig blackbottom shimmy
of generous racket. This was how we whooped it up
when she poured and sifted and melted herself through the air.

Look my love, we hollered to ourselves in her voice.
We have no i, the world our mind, the world is one.
Yes, mother, we bellowed back to her in all her other souls and
                                                    instruments.

This is what we are for.

Before Notre Dame:

WHATEVER I'VE TAKEN   *Sonnet*

WHATEVER i've taken i'll give back again   *a*
though changed—my body to your waiting earth   *b*
in hope that time will mend, not make me worse   *b*
while filtering out my hard parts as the best;   *c*
my eyes cleaned out and carved to make this pen, *a*
the corners dripping ink still when, inert,   *b*
the mind lies rotten; my dead marriage berthed   *b*
long years where wasted things can be at rest;   *c*
and this—your love that wrote me, blazed my slate *d*
with promise, as before the Mother's gate   *d*
her saints stand naked, paint and pride washed clean *e*
while on her roof their brothers / sisters wait   *d*
silent when rain, when air dissolves their straight *d*
and sombre coats of bronze to leaping green.   *e*

85

BIOGRAPHICAL NOTE

JUDITH JOHNSON is the author of six previously published books of poetry and one of short fiction. Her first book, *Uranium Poems,* won the 1968 Yale Series of Younger Poets Prize. Later awards have included a *Playboy* fiction award, a National Endowment for the Arts Poetry Fellowship, and the Poetry Society of America Di Castagnola Prize. An intermedia and performance artist as well as a writer, Ms. Johnson originally planned to become an opera composer, and studied musical composition at Juilliard with Suzanne Bloch and Bernard Wagenaar. Her intermedia installation, "Friedrich Liebermann, American Artist," has been widely exhibited. Recently, with Brenda S. Webster, she has been coediting the journal of the late abstract expressionist artist, Ethel Schwabacher, due in 1993 from Indiana University Press. A former president of the Poetry Society of America, she is now editor of the feminist literary periodical *13th Moon,* and publisher of *The Little Magazine.* Before 1985, she published under the name Judith Johnson Sherwin. She teaches in the Women's Studies and graduate writing programs of the State University of New York at Albany, and is the mother of three daughters, Miranda, Alison and Galen.

POETRY FROM THE SHEEP MEADOW PRESS

Desire for White
Allen Afterman (1991)

Early Poems
Yehuda Amichai (1983)

Travels
Yehuda Amichai (1986)

**Love Poems and
Jerusalem Poems**
Yehuda Amichai (1992)

Father Fisheye
Peter Balakian (1979)

Sad Days of Light
Peter Balakian (1983)

Reply from Wilderness Island
Peter Balakian (1988)

5 A.M. in Beijing
Willis Barnstone (1987)

Wheat Among Bones
Mary Baron (1979)

The Secrets of the Tribe
Chana Bloch (1980)

The Past Keeps Changing
Chana Bloch (1992)

Memories of Love
Bohdan Boychuk (1989)

Brothers, I Loved You All
Hayden Carruth (1978)

Orchard Lamps
Ivan Drach (1978)

A Full Heart
Edward Field (1977)

Stars in My Eyes
Edward Field (1978)

New and Selected Poems
Edward Field (1987)

Embodiment
Arthur Gregor (1982)

Secret Citizen
Arthur Gregor (1989)

Nightwords
Samuel Hazo (1987)

Leaving the Door Open
David Ignatow (1984)

The Flaw
Yaedi Ignatow (1983)

The Ice Lizard
Judith Johnson (1992)

The Roman Quarry
David Jones (1981)

Claims
Shirley Kaufman (1984)

Summers of Vietnam
Mary Kinzie (1990)

The Wellfleet Whale
Stanley Kunitz (1983)

The Moonlit Upper Deckerina
Naomi Lazard (1977)

OTHER TITLES

Kabbalah and Consciousness
Allen Afterman (1992)

Collected Prose
Paul Celan (1986)

Dean Cuisine
Jack Greenberg and
James Vorenberg (1990)

**The Notebooks of
David Ignatow**
David Ignatow (1984)

**A Celebration for
Stanley Kunitz**
Edited by Stanley Moss (1986)

**Interviews and Encounters
with Stanley Kunitz**
Edited by Stanley Moss (1992)

The Stove and Other Stories
Jakov Lind (1983)

Two Plays
Howard Moss (1980)

Arshile Gorky
Harold Rosenberg (1985)

Literature and the Visual Arts
Edited by Mark Rudman (1989)

**Stories and Recollections of
Umberto Saba**
Umberto Saba (1992)

The Tales of Arturo Vivante
Arturo Vivante (1990)

**Will the Morning Be Any
Kinder than the Night?**
Irving Wexler (1991)

**The Summers of James and
Annie Wright**
James and Annie Wright (1981)